HOW TO TRAIN
YOUR CAT

"Cuddly", "Loving" and "Clean" are three terms used by cat-lovers all over the world to describe their feline friends. Whilst "Conniving", "Lazy" and "Selfish" are used by those not so chummy with their pussies. But whichever point of view you take, everyone agrees "You can't train a cat".

WRONG !

In HOW TO TRAIN YOUR CAT, Dr Phee Line will show you how you can educate your moggie. Get it to perform simple tricks such as rolling over and begging, right through to 'high level' tasks like flying an aeroplane.

By careful selection of its natural abilities, you can make your cat perform a useful function around the house (for a change).

Memories of
Sooty, Teddy, Lewetor,
Samantha & Trouble

R&B is an imprint of:-
R&B Publishing
PO Box 200
Harrogate
HG2 9RB
England
Tel/Fax:(0423)507545

Australasian Edition:-
MaxiBooks
P.O.Box 268
Springwood
NSW 2777
Australia
Tel:(047)514967, Fax:(047)515545

Copyright © 1992 R&B Publishing

First Published in October 1992 by R&B Publishing

This book is a work of fiction and humour. Under no circumstances do the author, the publishers or anyone connected with this book advocate any form of cruelty towards a cat (or any other animal for that matter). You should not attempt to implement or follow any of the lessons or methods in this book.

ISBN 1-873668-05-8

Typesetting and design by:
Impact Designs, P.O.Box 200, Harrogate, HG2 9RB, England.

Illustrations by Kate Taylor.

Printed and bound in Spain by Grafos S.A., Barcelona.

British Library Cataloguing-in-Publication Data:
A catalogue record for this book is
available from the British Library

CONTENTS

Train Your Cat to

FIRST PRINCIPAWLES

While attempting to train your cat, you should bear in mind that all cats are curious, self-sufficient and manipulative.

No doubt your moggie currently has a very comfortable home with food provided at least twice a day. It doesn't need to lift a single whisker for itself. A few purrs and a couple of rubs up against your legs will keep you just where the cat wants you - under the paw.

It will be hard, but during the training period you must resist all such attempts by kitty to manipulate you. You are about to enter a phycological war with your cat. LOSE and you are condemned to a life of pussy pampering. WIN and you can sit back and relax as your cat starts attending to your needs for a change.

And don't worry about your moggie losing out. Cats have never allowed circumstances to come between them and a life of luxury. As you stop attending to your feline's every desire, its self-sufficiency will come to the fore. The less you do, the more your moggie will do for itself.

Dr Phee Line

Train Your Cat to

EAT WITH UTENSILS

Teaching your cat to eat may sound akin to showing Australians how to drink, instructing Americans to 'think big' and Educating the British to eat fish 'n' chips; it should come naturally. But would you invite your cat to the dinner table? And would you feel safe inviting your boss round for a meal with you and your cat?

The first aspect to tackle is volume. At present, if you put a bowl of food in front of your cat, it will probably gobble down the whole lot without coming up for a single breath. Alter this by placing the cat's food on a plate, letting it eat and then removing it when your moggie has taken two or three mouths-full. Wait a decent time, during which polite conversation can take place, then return the plate so pussy can have another nibble. Repeat this exercise until your feline leaves gaps between its gulps.

Making your cat use knives and forks is a little more difficult. The best way to approach this problem is by example. Start eating your own meals off a plate on the floor next to your cat's. Always use your knife and fork, and look disgusted each time your moggie pushes its face into the grub. Before long, pussy will have been shamed into using its own cutlery. Some owners will find they need to invest time in a few extra lessons to teach their cat which is the fork-paw and which is the knife-paw.

CAT

HANDY HINT:
*During this exercise,
you should also be
introducing two veg
onto the plate beside
the meat.*

FOOD

8

Train Your Cat to

SIT AT THE TABLE

Commence by serving your cat's food on the dinner table. The cat will have to jump onto a seat and then reach up to the table to eat it. Consuming the meal will now take it longer than a millisecond, because you've taught your pussy to take several polite pawses. So, before long, your moggie's back legs will begin to tire. When fatigue has completely taken over, you should find your feline friend in a sitting position on the seat.

Etiquette dictates lady cats should cross their legs when sitting. To encourage this sitting position, do not let your cat out or give it access to a litter tray for six hours before a meal. If it has gulped down a pint or two of milk in the morning it should become desperate for the toilet and cross its legs.

A side benefit of teaching your cat to use chairs is that it will sit in your favourite armchair. This will warm up the seat so you don't get a cold shock when you sit down. Don't be upset if your cat does not move immediately when you want to sit down. This is because it knows what temperature you like and is trying to tell you the seat is not yet warm enough.

CAT

HANDY HINT
Remember not to use your best chairs during this training period.

FOOD

Train Your Cat to

LIE DOWN

Falling down and going to sleep is one of the feline's strongest abilities. The problem is, they do it anywhere and everywhere, but always in the 'wrong' place. Many a broken leg can be attributed to a trip over a flaked-out moggie. Of course, some of these falls may be a deliberate attempt by kitty to get you to drop some food or spill some milk. So it is all the more important to instil some idea of when and where it should lie-down.

Some observers advocate giving the moggie a small kick if it goes to sleep in the wrong place. This is cruel; imagine how you would feel if you got a size twelve up your backside whenever you dozed-off in your favourite armchair. A better method is to:-

1)   Gently tap your cat on the shoulder, and indicate there is a juicy meal waiting for it in its own bed,

2)   Try picking up your feline friend, taking care not to wake it, and placing it in the required sleeping area, or

3)   Follow the cat around and when it is about to fall on the ground quickly push its bed underneath it. When the cat wakes, it will think it is always sleeping in the same place, get used to the idea and go there naturally.

13

Train Your Cat to

USE THE TOILET

by putting some cat litter in the toilet and
tying some wool to the handle

Train Your Cat to

KEEP YOUR ACCOUNTS

Not much training needed -
Cats are naturally conniving and can avoid most taxes

Train Your Cat to
STAND UP AND WALK

Again, on the face of it, there may not seem to be any problem getting cats to walk. However, they have a habit of either belting around like a streak of greased lightening or sauntering along as if they've had a heavy session on the cat-nip.

Place your cat in the middle of a room, walk to the side, and call it over for its food. If the cat rushes over, do not give it the food but simply take kitty back into the middle of the room. Repeat this exercise until the cat walks over in a sprightly but not too hurried manner.

Some cats will get hungry if you continue not to feed them. Consequently they'll start running over to you faster each time you call them for food. Combat this by standing behind your cat, so it has to walk backwards. This method should reverse the speeding-up process and gradually slow the cat down.

Why not ask a few friends round to your house to watch your cat walk. If you have prepared some scorecards beforehand, your friends can hold up their marks for each moggie promenade. To encourage your cat, ask your friends to cheer and clap when kitty does a really smart step.

CAT

HANDY HINT:
Go out and purchase a metronome. If you purr-sist long enough, you should be able to get your cat to walk in time with the clicks.

FOOD

16

Cats usually try to run before they can walk

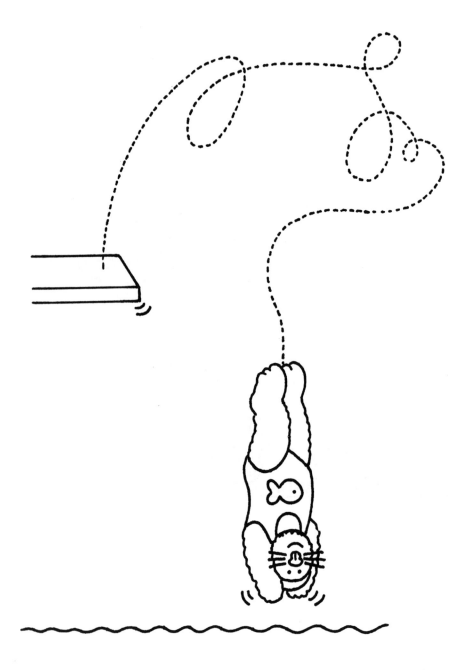

Train Your Cat to
ROLL OVER

Use one of the three methods below to make your cat roll over while it is sleeping or resting. At the same time as kitty makes a move you should say "Roll Over" in a firm, but not too loud, voice. Your cat will then become conditioned to the rolling action when you issue your command.

1) Use a feather to tickle kitty's nose. At first, the moggie might try to remove the source of irritation by bringing its paws up. Since it won't open its eyes, this should not affect the training programme. Keep tickling and the cat will eventually roll over to get away from the nuisance.

2) Reflect the sun off your watch onto its eye-lids. The brightness should make your pussy either roll over or get up and draw the curtains*. At night-time you can use a strong lamp or spotlight.

3) Make your cat sleep on a wide mat. When it is asleep, carefully lift one end of the mat and keep going until the cat is rolled over. Go to the other end of the mat and repeat the exercise.

*If this happens at such an early stage of training your cat is showing great potential. You might want to consider jumping straight on to more difficult tricks.

HANDY HINT:
*For method one:
Wear a plastic apron
in case your cat
sneezes.*

Train Your Cat to

CLEAN YOUR WINDOWS

by spraying black paint on your windows - Cats are so inquisitive
they will clean the windows to see what is going on outside

Train Your Cat to

FIX YOUR CAR

Complain of a squeaking noise coming from the engine.
Your moggie will then dismantle it to find the mouse.

WASH ITSELF

Cats are intuitively clean creatures, but they are also extremely lazy. Given the choice of having a bath or lying in the sun, the average moggie will always choose the solar option. To go up to the bathroom and get in the tub is simply too much effort. So most kitties make do with a quick lick each day.

To overcome this you must take all psychological obstacles away from in front of your cat. Make going for a bath really easy and try to make it fun. Try running the bath and dangling a plastic mouse on the end of a piece of string in the water. If you can't find a mouse, use goldfish. Both of these methods should tempt puss into the water.

When experienced and short of time, your cat will probably prefer a shower. Get kitty used to showering by leaving it out in the rain for short periods. When it has its first real shower, use one of the less powerful models where the cat will have to run around in order to get wet.

You should also leave some toothpaste in the bathroom for your cat to clean its teeth. Female cats may wish to make use of some make-up. Leave this on the side and kitty will probably cover its fur in the powder. The fur will then become matted and it will need another bath, thereby getting it used to washing.

CAT

HANDY HINT:
Cats are very vain;
always make sure there
are at least two
mirrors for the cat to
admire itself after
washing.

FOOD

22

MEEOWWWW

24

Train Your Cat to

JUMP OVER OBJECTS

Before tackling objects, you should concentrate on simply getting your cat to jump. Although most felines are used to jumping up to catch birds, to get onto their favourite chair or to come and sit on your lap, they are not used to jumping for the fun of it.

Wait until your cat is asleep and creep up behind it. Reach down behind it and clap your hands loudly near its ears. The cat should then jump. If your moggie is slightly deaf you may need to burst a paper bag to achieve the desired effect. White cats are sometimes partially deaf which can be a problem, so you may need to purchase a starting pistol plus blanks.

When the cat is in mid-jump, pass a rope or thin stick underneath its body. The cat will still be surprised at the noise and think it is moving and not the rope or stick.

Advance by putting your moggies food or a toy mouse on the opposite side of a perspex sheet. The cat will be able to see the food and very soon figure out it has to jump the obstacle to get fed.

After a few months jumping, you should take your cat along to a three-day event. By watching the horses, kitty will be able to improve its jumping techniques and practice for when cat-jumping becomes an olympic demonstration sport.

CAT

HANDY HINT
Jumping with a full stomach may be difficult, so remove the perspex after the first jump.

FOOD

Train Your Cat to

PLAY DARTS

Don't be worried about the sharp points,
your moggie's claws are a lot sharper.

Train Your Cat to

BRING YOUR SLIPPERS

Let your cat overhear a conversation in which you say the dog is
your favourite because it brings your slippers to you.

BEG

Being proud creatures, cats don't generally like to be seen begging. Start training in the privacy of your own home during the cat's feeding time. When pussy trots over for its food, hold the bowl around one to two feet above the ground. Your moggie will initially be confused, but will eventually go up on its hind legs to see into the bowl - this is the classic begging position.

When the begging posture has become natural, take the bowl away and replace it with a flat cloth cap. You can then send the cat out onto the streets with the cap to do a bit of begging. You will find the extra cash handy to pay for the cat's food.

If you want to go on an exotic holiday, you can improve the moggies income by putting one of its paws in a pretend sling or using a false eye-patch. The additional sympathy will lead to larger donations in the cap.

If your feline totally refuses to go out begging, train it to play the guitar. One or two nights busking can bring in as much money as a whole week of sticking the paw out. Warning: Do not attempt to train your cat to play the violin, it might get upset at the sight of the strings.

CAT

HANDY HINT

Make sure you register the cat for income tax, or else its earnings may be added to yours.

FOOD

Train Your Cat to

TELL THE TIME

Before moving on to clocks as humans know them, you will need to work on the cat's body clock. Always feed your moggie at the same time in the morning and evening. Kitty will soon realise what is happening and start watching the clock to know when to start hassling your for the grub.

Ivan Pavlov used a bell to condition a dog into knowing when its food was going to be served. Therefore, you might find that a clock which chimes every hour will help your moggie keep track of the time. A cuckoo clock is ideal because the noise wakes the cat, and the little cuckoo reminds the pussy of food.

Progress on to a clock with symbols instead of numbers. This will test if your cat is really telling the time or if it is remembering the numbers. Finally try altering the clocks to tell the wrong time. Cats who have learnt to tell the time properly will consult their watches and know what the real time is. A cat which is too clever will demand food anyway, on the grounds that it is feeding time in some other part of the world.

CAT
HANDY HINT
Noddy clocks interest cats but have the side effect of developing a pathological hatred of red cars, blue hats and people with big ears.

FOOD

Train Your Cat to

BLOW UP BALLOONS

Buy some gloves so your cat's claws don't burst the balloons

Train Your Cat to

GUARD YOUR HOUSE

Cats are good at guarding houses
unless you suffer from cat-burglars

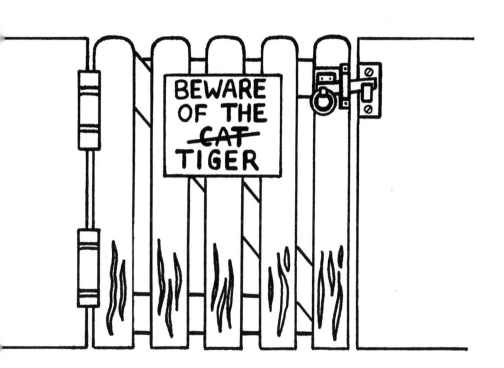

Train Your Cat to

READ BOOKS AND NEWSPAPERS

Most cats can already read street names and door numbers. How else do you think they can find their way back home. So you need to develop this existing ability.

As ever, start at feeding time. Buy two bowls, and write "Cat" on one and "Dog" on the other. Then put cat food in the 'cat' bowl and cabbage in the 'dog' bowl. Your moggie will read which bowl belongs to it and go to that bowl. Note that it may look as if your cat is sniffing the food but it is actually getting close enough to read the writing.

Develop your cat's vocabulary by putting down several brands of feline fodder. It will read each can and make its choice based upon the nutritional information contained on the label.

CAT

HANDY HINT

Make sure you read the newspapers as well. Otherwise, your cat may become a better conversationalist than you are at parties.

FOOD

One cat year is the equivalent to seven human years. You can use this factor to determine the effective reading age of your moggie and to decide which books to buy it. When you give new books to your feline, hand them over upside-down to see if it is really reading or just pretending.

Cats also like newspapers. If you can stop kitty jumping into the middle of the paper and ripping it to shreds, your feline should pick up on current affairs. Older cats like to read the Financial Times so they can keep track of their stocks and shares.

Train Your Cat to

WRITE LETTERS

Pour some water-soluble ink into a shallow tray and put it on the floor. Then persuade your pussy to walk through it in the usual manner by putting food or a toy mouse on the other side. As the cat steps out of the ink, put some quality writing paper underneath its paws. The resulting mess may not look like a letter you would want to receive, but it will mean something to another cat.

As your cat gets used to writing letters in this manner, start to put a toy mouse in the ink. The moggie should try to pull the mouse out using only its claws. A much more legible letter should result, with the cat's claws being used in the same manner as a quill. The individual words will be more legible because the rest of the paw is not causing a smudge, so your kitty might start to receive some replies to its mailings.

Your feline will soon grow tired of the replies it is getting and will want to communicate with a different set of cats. Place an advert for claw-friends in a magazine, or get your cat to do it. Although your cat may be able to write and address letters, it will need some help with affixing the stamps. Try putting some fish oil onto the sticky part of the stamp so the cat licks it before putting it on the envelope.

CAT
HANDY HINT
Remember to wipe your pussy's paws before it steps off the paper, otherwise it could create an unwanted work of art on your new carpet.

FOOD

COOK FOR ITSELF

Encourage your cat to take up cooking by presenting it with poor or unimaginative food. Become totally repetitive in what you give it, and invest in at least two months supply of the same flavour. After a week of identical dishes, leave the door to the cupboard slightly open. Your moggie won't be able to resist looking through the gap. When it sees row upon row of the same flavour, it will rush into the kitchen to start cooking for itself.

Make sure there are plenty of fresh items around for it to create a variety of interesting dishes, so you can get it hooked. The thought of returning to all those tins should mean that you never have to prepare another meal for your moggie. Also arrange for a cat-sized apron and hat to be available. Just like humans, moggies do not like to find unwanted fur in their dishes.

A trip to the local bookshop could prove useful. Search out a couple of titles on cordon-purr and nouvelle-pussine, to keep your kitty's culinary imagination going. In the long term, you should give your cat a gastronomic aim. Enter it into a cookery competition and take it along to audiences for cookery programmes.

CAT

HANDY HINT

Make some extra cash by getting your cat to open a cake stall at local coffee mornings or church fêtes

FOOD

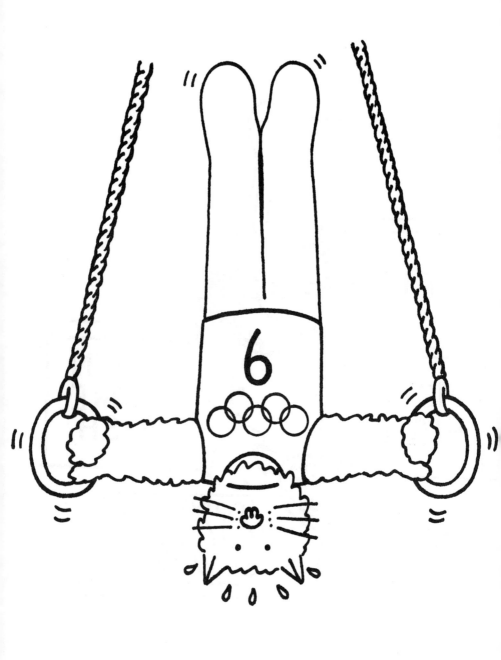

Train Your Cat to

DO FRONT PAW STANDS

A hand-stand is a difficult trick for a human to perform. But the equivalent feat is slightly easier for cats who have a better sense of balance. Whilst a cat's rear legs are strong enough to propel it over any obstacles between it and it's food, the front legs are not so muscular. In order to build up the front paw power, hold your cat's back paws in the air for short periods. Take care not to over-do this exercise, or else moggie will become dizzy and form an aversion to inversion.

When the muscles are brawny enough for front paw stands, encourage your kitty to develop some stamina by holding it's food bowl upside down. Being inquisitive and ever hopeful, your cat will perform a front paw stand to see if there is anything in the dish and stay there in the belief that something will spontaneously arrive.

Cartwheels, flips and spins should be the next aim for your feline. Don't forget to provide encouragement in the form of applause when your cat tries a new manoeuvre. A couple of small falls can knock a moggies ego, so your support will help. A mirror installed on the wall will help correct any errors in execution. As kitty advances in calisthenic complexity, you will find its sessions in the training gymnasium an ideal way to keep small children amused.

CAT

HANDY HINT
*Buy your cat a tutu
for protection of its
dignity.*

FOOD

41

Train Your Cat to

DIG THE GARDEN

One thing which irks most moggies is the fact that dogs generally make better hole diggers than cats. Although felines practice their burrowing when they use the toilet, they usually achieve nothing more than a hollow impression in the soil. You can overcome this in two easy stages. Firstly provide a target for your moggie by burying a fish bone or can of cat food in the garden. Secondly give it a shovel so it doesn't have to dirty its paws.

You can save on the cost of other garden implements by getting your cat to rake the top soil with its claws. The individual claws are perfectly spaced to remove any undesired small stones and bits of broken glass. If your cat has sharp talons, you can save on a lawn-mower by getting moggie to walk over the grass with its claws out, moving its paws in a scything motion. Really well honed nails can be used to prune roses.

CAT

HANDY HINT

When sending your cat out to work in the garden, warn the local bird population by placing advertisements in the local press and making announcements on the radio.

FOOD

The tail is also a useful implement for sweeping leaves into piles ready for burning. Take care to keep your cat out of the way when setting fire to the mound. Most moggies don't know how to use matches and they might set fire to your house by mistake.

Don't forget cats are good climbers. If your tree needs trimming, send your moggie up with a chain-saw because it will have a good head for heights.

 42

Train Your Cat to

OPEN TIN CANS

by leaving a tin of cat food on the floor. Your resourceful cat
will find a way of opening it.

Train Your Cat to

DO AS YOU COMMAND

by telling the cat to do the opposite of what you want

Train Your Cat to

PUT THE MILK BOTTLES OUT

As far as your cat is concerned the milk appears from your fridge. So, the first step you must undertake is to educate it into knowing where the milk bottles come from. Try not giving your moggie any milk for a few days. It will soon get a craving for some of the white nectar and go in search. Of course, once your cat has started bringing the milk into the house, you should give it a percentage of the take. Put, say, a third of the bottle's contents into its bowl.

Empty bottles should be washed and put into the cats favourite sleeping place. At first kitty will ignore them and sleep slightly over to one side. But as the number of bottles increases, it will get upset and look for somewhere else to put them. Unless your cat is particularly thick, it should remember where the bottles came from in the morning and put them back there.

HANDY HINT
Fit one of those locks which fastens when the door closes, so the cat automatically puts itself out at the same time.

To save you opening the door for your cat to put the bottles out, why not fix a cat-flap. Make sure the opening is large enough to get the bottles out, or you may find a frustrated pile of broken glass in the morning.

Training your cat to write notes for the milkman can save you more effort when you want an extra pint. But be careful when you go on holiday. You may find your cat will order ten pints for itself every day.

Train Your Cat to

LEAVE BIRDS ALONE

Birds have an annoying habit of poking fun at our feline friends. Just listen carefully to birdsong at the crack of dawn; "Have you heard the one about the bird, the dog and the cat...". This is why most moggies love nothing better than to pluck a few feathers from their teeth.

Get up early one morning and have a quiet word with some of the birds' leaders. Explain you are trying to train your cat not to attack birds and ask for their help. If amenable, persuade them to tweet something complimentary about your moggie when they know it is listening. Combine this friendly feather strategy with a trip to a feline psychologist to give your cat a sense of self belief.

Unless you are convinced your kitty has stopped killing birds, it is strongly recommended that you set up a video recording system in your garden. Many moggies continue to commit their terrible acts and hide or bury the incriminating evidence. If this happens, replay the video proof when your cat makes any denials in an attempt to shame it into giving up completely.

Converted cats can help the birds to build nests and join in the construction of bird-tables. Further fulfilment can be obtained by employing your cat as a feather-check attendant at bird-bath parties.

CAT

HANDY HINT
Another way of getting your cat to kick the chirper chewing habit is to take it along to a hypnocatapist.

FOOD

Train Your Cat to

DELIVER MAIL

Start sending your letters to a cat food factory or fish factory.

Train Your Cat to

LIFT WEIGHTS

by putting your cat in a wet paper bag and seeing
if it can get out.

Train Your Cat to

GO ON A DIET

Felines are well known for their love of food and their desire to bite anything that moves. So don't expect to get kitty on a diet simply by suggesting it. You must work from a more subtle angle.

Leave slimming magazines around the house and use the centre pages in the cat litter tray or under the food bowls. Start talking about fat cats and how you don't like them. Mention a few things which you know your cat would like to do but can't quite manage due to the over-sized gut. And finally, pat your stomach with both hands every time you stand up, and look meaningfully towards your moggie.

If your cat still isn't convinced it should cut down on its weight, you will have to try more devious methods. Obtain a distortion mirror which makes moggie look gross around the midriff. Also take some photographs of your cat posing in the sun. Then take them to your local specialist and get him to doctor the images by adding a chin or two and a couple of inches of blubber.

CAT

HANDY HINT
Keep a log of your cat's calorific intake so it can educate itself into eating less.

FOOD

There is bound to be a slimming club in your area. They will be able to help your moggie, and it won't be bothered by the catty remarks it might receive from the other members. Give kitty some incentives by sponsoring it for every pound it loses. Also, don't forget the standard 'before and after' photographs for possible promotion work.

Cats don't like diets.

PICK UP FUR

No doubt your cat is adept at leaving its fur around the house, but not so good at picking it up, particularly during the moulting period. This is because it has never bothered the cat. After all, it has washed the fur every day so it can't be dirty.

Go along to a scientific laboratory and ask if you can borrow one of their microscopes. Take it home and train the lens on a clump of discarded fur. When in focus, call your cat over to examine the evidence. It should be able to make out the many thousands of cat-fur bugs which live in such heaps. Revulsion should make moggie rush to the cupboard and pull out the vacuum cleaner.

If there is no response to the above method, tickle your cats nose with some of its fur when it is trying to sleep. Get a leaflet from the vet on the subject of feline hygiene and leave it on the cat's bed. Then start putting clumps of mouse fur in kitty's food and milk. It will soon get the hint.

The easiest way for your cat to pick up its fur, if it doesn't own a vacuum, is by attaching sticky tape to its paws. As it walks around the house, individual hairs will stick to the tape and be pulled off your carpet.

Advanced cats can be trained to change the filter on your washing machine to prevent blockages.

CAT

HANDY HINT
*Collect the discarded fur
and use it to knit
yourself a warm jumper
for the cooler months.*

FOOD

55

Train Your Cat to

PEEL AND SLICE POTATOES

Put a small pair of plastic ears and a tail on your potatoes, then leave them under your sofa.

Train Your Cat to

BALANCE A BALL ON ITS NOSE

by throwing it some fish when it is successful.

Train Your Cat to

SING

Leaving a cat out at night can prompt a late night or early morning serenade. But it is more likely to be the sort of song which will result in the throwing of an old boot than the tapping of feet. This is because most humans do not appreciate a moggy's choice of music.

Change your pussy's taste in music by playing it your favourite tapes or CDs throughout the day. If your own appetite is for particularly loud or rapid music, be careful not to damage your cat's hearing. Gently place a soft toy mouse in each of its ears.

Music lessons might be a help, but you should certainly buy some sheet music to help your cat with the basics. If you are musically inclined yourself, accompany your moggie on the piano as it practices its scales. Don't forget to make a tape recording of its songs, so it can hear afterwards what each harmony sounded like.

There could be benefits of a different kind in the shape of a recording contract. Cut a few tracks, using your cats claws if you are short of cash. Then send some demo tapes to radio stations and recording companies. You never know, you could see your moggie's songs cat-apulting into the charts.

CAT

HANDY HINT
Make sure you get a water proof recording contract because cats don't like H_2O.

FOOD

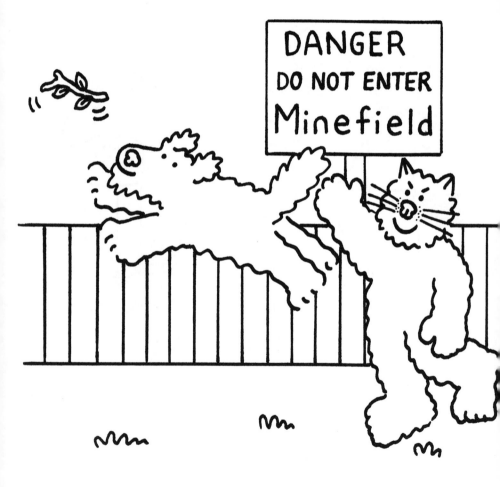

Train Your Cat to

TAKE THE DOG FOR A WALK

A common misconception is that dogs chase cats. Actually, the cats are taking the dogs for a stroll. If there was any maliciousness involved, the cat would stand its ground and have a sharp word with the dog. Not many canines will face up to a spitting, hissing ball of fur with razor sharp claws.

Impress upon your moggie that the walks should be taken in a more controlled manner, so as not to damage too many plants in the garden and cause too many cars to leave the road. Give your kitty a lead with which it can control the dog. One which retracts at the press of a button is recommended, so the cat can keep closer control over its charge. A slip knot lead is not advised just in case the moggie takes a dislike to Rover.

Encourage your cat to take the dog along when it goes shopping by giving it some money to stop at the pub on the way back. Also reward it when it brings the mutt back. This will stop pussy 'accidentally' leaving the dog chained to a parked car or simply letting it go.

As the relationship between your dog and your cat progresses you may want to take the training a step further. Look in your local press to see if there are any dog obedience lessons starting. If there are, why not send your cat along with your dog one night?

CAT

HANDY HINT
You may need to put blinkers on your dog so it doesn't notice other dogs laughing at it.

FOOD

Train Your Cat to

DRIVE A CAR

Before you let your cat out onto the roads with a real car, you will need to teach it some road sense. Children's toy cars are ideal for this. Let your cat push the toys around with its paws, encouraging it to try several models from sports cars through to stationwagens.

Continue training by taking your cat out on a bicycle. This will increase its road 'awareness'. Go out early in the morning if you live in a busy area so your pussy doesn't get frightened.

When you progress onto a real car you will need to make a few adjustments. A pillow or two on the drivers seat will help your moggie see where it is going. You will also have to remove the windscreen wipers, because you may find the car swerving out of control when the cat tries to catch them going from side to side. Use a car with a cat-alytic converter. This device automatically corrects the car's characteristics for your cat.

An old aerodrome is an ideal place to let kitty get used to the controls. But, when you go on to the open road, watch out for any dogs going for a walk. Your moggie will be prone to leaving the road and chasing the hound at full speed. Make sure you have a good insurance policy and name the cat as a driver.

CAT

HANDY HINT

Always inform the police that your cat was in charge of the car if you receive a parking or speeding fine through the post.

FOOD

Train Your Cat to

USE A COMPUTER

To fully appreciate the power of a computer your cat should be able to do arithmetic by more conventional means. Make an abacus from balls of wool. Your cat will play with them, and will be able to keep a tally of its number of meals. For training with higher numbers, it can count the number of hours sleep it has each day.

As a further step you should let your cat do its own shopping. Using money will get it used to all four functions of addition, subtraction, division and multiplication. Don't be surprised if your moggie asks for a calculator to keep track of all the special offers.

You can introduce your cat to a keyboard with the use of fish oil on the keys you want it to press. Let it play games on the computer with lots of colourful graphics; 'Canine Invaders' is a favourite with computer literate moggies. You should buy a mouse and pad for your cat to save it using the cursor keys.

Later on, your cat will use business packages to keep track of its savings and as a stock control on its food reserves. Watch out for signs of your moggie hacking into other computer systems. Cats are extremely stealthy and can move around a system without being noticed.

HANDY HINT
Find out your cat's puss-word so you can keep track of its computing activities.

Train Your Cat to

DO AEROBICS

Cut a piece of string or wool and tempt your cat into playing with it on the floor. Once the cat is interested, drag the string rhythmically from side to side, then pull it towards you and push it away. Repeat each direction ten times slowly.

Obtain a small rubber ball and bounce it against the wall. Your cat will chase it along the ground, keeping low, and then jump into the air when it rebounds.

When kitty is ready to enrol into a professional aerobics class, you must make sure it is dressed properly. Make or buy a leotard with some fetching stripes - simulated leopard-skin would look in place - and don't forget to varnish your cat's claws in an attractive pink. If you can, find some short socks with bobbles on the back. These will keep all the other cats in the class occupied during the slower exercises.

CAT

HANDY HINT
If you remove the bells, your cat can use its collar as a trendy headband.

FOOD

There may be a tendency for your pussy to show off in the class. It will be far more flexible and definitely fitter than any of the other members, especially during the high-impact aerobic sessions. Moggies street cred may be damaged, though, if its mascara runs and mats its fur.

Don't expect kitty home straight after the class. The different cliques will probably retire to the local hostelry for a pint of milk and some catty talk about the inabilities the human members.

Train Your Cat to

SAVE MONEY

Give your cat a mouse-bank in which to save its coins
(a piggy bank would be too big).

Train Your Cat to

RETRIEVE

by throwing the cat's food bowl out into the garden.

Train Your Cat to

PARACHUTE

Most moggies have an extremely good head for heights. They are also very adept at landing on their feet no matter from what height they've fallen. These skills will help your pussy develop a natural 'roll' when it lands by parachute.

Sometimes cats get stuck in trees, but this is purely due to a lack of confidence in throwing itself off high objects without a good reason. Try attaching small pieces of its favourite food to leaves during the spring. When they fall off later in the year, your kitty will jump after them.

You can also indulge in some indoor training by getting your moggie to jump off the wardrobe onto the bed. When it has gained some confidence, you can attach a handkerchief to its back with four short strings. You can simulate the carrying of a 'chute on its back by pushing a small lunchbox underneath the back of its T-shirt.

When your feline is a proficient parachutist, it can put on displays at local fêtes and church fund raising afternoons. A favourite with the crowds is when your moggie lands on a two inch toy mouse from a height of 10,000 feet. Keep an eye on the press, you could read about your pussy performing a daring raid to free fellow felines from captivity in boarding kennels.

CAT

HANDY HINT
Tie a lipstick to one of its back paws so it leaves a red trail as it flies through the air.

FOOD

Train Your Cat to

FLY A PLANE

Next time you go to the supermarket, take a bag full of small coins and your cat with you. In front of the shop you will find some 'rides' for small children. One of these is usually in the shape of an aeroplane, and it goes backwards and forwards when you put a coin in the slot. Let your moggie have a go and get used to the idea of being in a plane. You should do this only after you have been shopping; one of the plastic bags may come in handy if your pussy gets air sick.

Make your cat a flying suit with helmet and goggles. Swimming hats and goggles are ideal if you can't find any real aviators head gear. When smartly dressed up, take your kitty down to the nearest airline office and get it a job as an in-flight attendant.

Between flights you can familiarise your cat with the processes of flying the aircraft itself. Buy it a cockpit lay-out jigsaw so it can get used to the position of the different controls. Also invest in a 'Teach Yourself Landing Techniques' manual, and test your cat every evening.

CAT

HANDY HINT
Don't let your cat fly too far or it may face three months in quarantine when it returns.

FOOD

You may find a trip to an air show worthwhile, and you could pay for your pussy to have a trip in a helicopter or glider. You may find your cat gets a craving for the air and wants to go hang-gliding. If this happens, you can save cash by making the glider from a kite and the harness from a pair of old trouser belts.

Train Your Cat to

PLAY FOOTBALL

by enrolling your cat in a team called 'Lions', 'Panthers', 'Cougars' or something similar.

Train Your Cat to

SLEEP LESS

Purchase a long-playing video of exotic fish in a tank
and keep replaying it.

Train Your Cat to

SKI

The only thing cats like about snow is chasing the snowflakes as they fall from the sky. Otherwise they hate cold weather, especially if their paws get wet and start to freeze. Knit your cat a very warm jacket and trousers before you send it outside. Don't forget to consult some fashion magazines to make sure you are using 'this years colours'.

Acclimatise your pussy to moving around on snow by putting it on the back of a sledge and pulling it around your garden or a field.

Skis and ski-poles can be fashioned from plastic knives and forks for when your cat is ready to start skiing downhill. If you want it to concentrate on slalom, you should wind some string between the poles and put a toy mouse on the end. When your cat sets off, pull the mouse through the gate poles and your cat should follow.

Your moggie may take to the snow like a duck to water. In which case it may want four skis instead of two, so it can try some freestyle (also known as hot dogging, but don't tell your cat). It may also want to try aerial catrobatics and ski-jumping.

Your cat's favourite ski area will probably be Kittysbühel in Austria. The lift pass is quite expensive, but don't buy one for your pussy because its sense of balance will enable it to walk along the wire.

CAT

HANDY HINT
You should not use huskies to pull the sledge.

FOOD

"No - I said CUT !"

Train Your Cat to

TAKE PHOTOS

Secure your cat's interest in your camera by putting it on timed exposure and leaving it on the floor. Your cat will not be able to resist investigating where the 'clicking' noise is coming from. When it is close to the camera it will probably take a look through the viewfinder. If you have previously glued a small picture of a mouse onto the lens, it will be hooked on photography from then on.

Prepare kitty for the bright explosions of light when it uses the flash gun by rapidly switching your house lights on and off. Develop its artistic viewpoint by showing it glamour pictures of pussies of the opposite sex in fur raising positions.

The cat is used to climbing walls and fences. So it should be very good at getting a good position for unusual shots. It should also be able to cope with the crushes that always surround photo-opportunities with politicians and royalty.

Before long, your moggie will be able to build up an impressive purr-folio. And it may be able to land a job at one of the major newspapers as a pa-purr-azzi, or with a fashion house in Paris as a mode moggie.

CAT

HANDY HINT
Make sure your pussy does not put its paws over the lens or get fur on the film.

FOOD

Train Your Cat to

PLAY CHESS

by putting black and white carpet squares in your kitchen and
moving the cat food bowl around.

Train Your Cat to

DISCO DANCE

by heating your tin roof.

Train Your Cat to
MAKE A PHONE CALL

Leave your phone off the hook. The cat's acute hearing will pick up the purring sound of the dialling tone and come to investigate.

The next day, arrange to stay on late at work. The cat will get hungry and eagerly wait for your arrival. You can then call up to tell it you are going to be home late. Don't be put off if your feline doesn't answer straight away. Just stay at work until it becomes hungry enough to answer. If you then tell it where it can find some food, it will realise that it can get useful information from the 'phone.

The cat will soon want to make its own call, probably to remind you to bring its favourite fish home with you. To help it, you should make sure your 'phone is one of the push button variety because cats soon scratch the numbers off the dial models.

HANDY HINT

Double check veterinary appointments just before you leave the house; unscrupulous cats have been known to call up and cancel them.

A portable 'phone will be useful for your cat. If it gets caught out in the rain on its wanderings, it can call and ask you to come and pick it up. Note that it may experience difficulty with reception if there is any metal or a bell on its collar.

Arrange to receive a listing of the numbers you have called with your future telephone bills. This should alert you if pussy starts spending too much time on the 'phone to feline friends or ordering home deliveries of kippers.

"Hello, is that the local dog pound?"

Another delivery of cat food arrives safely.

Train Your Cat to
GO TO THE SUPERMARKET

It is easy to get your cat to go to the supermarket to get its own food, but more difficult for anything else. Try telling it what a large range of goods are available. Explain to your kitty that it could find grooming kits (brushes), home crafts (balls of wool) and cosmetics (flea powder).

When moggie has decided to make a shopping trip, you should surreptitiously insert some of your own items on the list. Hopefully your pussy will be so engrossed in what it is doing that it will bring home your needs without even noticing.

On the first trip, you will have to follow your cat and ask someone to step on the automatic door opener so the cat can get in. Once in the supermarket, the cat will not react favourably to a squeaking shopping trolley. Instead, it will probably run madly around the shop, and then report the owners to the health authorities for having mice.

Allow a long time before starting to get worried about your kitty's late return. Moggie will probably spend hours looking at the different cans of food and will not be able to pull itself away from the fish counter. It should not, however, have any difficulty getting an item from the top shelf. It will simply jump up and walk along the shelving.

CAT

HANDY HINT

Open a credit account so your cat does not get arrested for walking out without paying.

FOOD

Train Your Cat to

WHISTLE

You humm it, and your cat will whistle it.

Train Your Cat to

PAINT

Cats can only manage abstract paintings.

GO FISHING

Cats love fish but have absolutely no idea how to go about catching them; which is just as well or there would be no fish left anywhere in the world. As far as your moggie is concerned, all things fishy come from a tin or a supermarket.

You can combat these misconceptions by purchasing a child's fishing game. These games consist of plastic fish with metal rings in their mouths and a fishing rod with a magnet on the end of the line. Pussy can then practice in the comfort of its own home and get used to the idea of catching its own fish.

The time will come when you are ready to progress to the river bank. Make sure your moggie is well fed before you set off, otherwise you may find your catches disappearing as fast as you land them. It is also worthwhile making your cat dress up in a disguise so the fish don't get too frightened. Cats like chasing flies, so finding some fish bait should not be a problem.

Extra preparation will be required if you are planning to go fishing from a boat. Test your pussy's sea-legs by serving its food on a rocking chair every day for a week before your trip - green cats should not be taken on the trip.

CAT

FOOD

HANDY HINT
Make sure you put a secure cover on your goldfish pond in the garden.

COLLECT STAMPS

You should aim to capture your cat's philatelic imagination by purchasing some brightly coloured stamps from obscure African nations. These usually feature exotic birds and the odd jungle rodent - ideal for whetting moggie's appetite.

Very soon you will find it difficult to pull your feline away from its new hobby. If you drop a letter or an old envelope, your pussy will immediately pounce on it and rip it to shreds to get at the stamp. You may also find your moggie messing around in the neighbourhoods rubbish bins looking for discarded collectibles.

Like most collectors, your cat will find a philatelic speciality. This is likely to include stamps from Catalonia in Spain, Moggydishu in Somalia and Pussan in Korea. You will also notice your feline will be very precise with its collection, putting everything into categories and constantly refurring to its catalogues.

A recurring problem with this hobby is stopping your cat licking the backs of the stamps. But this should be outweighed by the advantages of sharp eyesight for spotting potentially financially lucrative errors on standard issues.

CAT

HANDY HINT
*Cats find it hard to pick
up stamps, so buy it
some tweezers.*

FOOD

Train Your Cat to
JUGGLING

Surprise your cat as it walks into the kitchen for its food by throwing it a full un-opened can. Then, before it can gather its composure throw it another can... and then another. At this point, your cat is likely to drop all three cans and walk away for a lie down to calm its nerves. But before it can do this, keep the pressure up by demanding which flavour it wants for its meal. The confused feline will then have to juggle the three cans between its paws in order to read the labels.

Watch your cat carefully as it juggles the cans, and when it looks like it has made a decision in favour of 'Tasty Tuna', throw in a can opener. Assuming your cat hasn't had a nervous breakdown by this stage, throw its food bowl into the mélange. Your cat will now be juggling five items, which is the limit with only two front paws.

CAT

HANDY HINT
If you find yourself a bit short on money, get your cat to juggle your finances.

FOOD

You may choose to let your feline have a rest at this stage - after all, it has just learnt a completely new trick in just a few seconds when it was only coming for a quiet snack. More adventurous owners can try adding a bowl of milk and a bowl of water, so their cats stand on one back paw and use the other three to juggle with. As a finale, stand behind your moggie and toss a whole fish up between its legs so it catches it in its mouth. Don't forget to give your cat plenty of applause and pass a cap round the kitchen for monetary contributions.

Train Your Cat to

LEARN LANGUAGES

The first language you should try to teach your cat is English. This may sound easy, but it is more difficult than you would think due to the number of different accents in both Pussy and English. In order to get your cat conversant with the distinct intonations, arrange a party and invite a wide range of friendly felines. You will need some Gutter Cats at the party so your moggie can learn to understand the pronunciation of different social classes. They can be a bit rough, especially after a pint or two of milk, so employ a large Tom on the door.

When your cat is fluent in all tones of English, it will be ready to learn a few foreign languages. Introduce it to a French Poodle, a German Dachshund and a Great Dane. Once these new friends have overcome their initial inhibitions, which may surface in the form of a lot of barking and chasing around, they will learn one another's tongues.

Improvements to your cat's foreign grammar can be achieved by enroling it in a cat correspondence course. Catsette tapes are used as aids to learning the spoken words, so make sure you buy your feline a walk-moggie. To bring the language 'alive', encourage your cat to write to overseas claw-friends and go on visits to them.

CAT

HANDY HINT
If your cat seems inept at languages, tell it to speak in English v-e-r-y s-l-o-w-l-y and L-O-U-D-L-Y.

FOOD

95

Train Your Cat to
KEEP THE HOUSE CLEAN

Pile everything that belongs to the cat - mats, food bowls, toys, etc. - into its favourite sleeping box. Then go and clean the brush which you use to keep your moggie's coat in good condition, and drop the fur onto its possessions. If you come across a couple of fleas, throw those in as well. Try and make it look like a real pigsty.

Being a sensitive creature, the cat should then take the hint and set about spring cleaning its retreat. Ensure that a vacuum cleaner and duster are available for your moggie to clean its box and the immediate surrounding area. You may want to allocate a couple of draws in some cupboards for your cat to put things in and maintain general tidiness.

CAT

HANDY HINT
Keep moving the box so
your cat ends up
cleaning the whole
house.

FOOD

Provide some environmentally friendly washing powder for your cat to wash its clothes with. Most moggies enjoy watching the garments going round and round in the washing machine. They also find it easy to put the items out onto the clothes line, because they can walk along the line putting in the pegs with their tails. This activity has the side benefit of giving your cat a chance to gossip with the neighbouring moggies. By carefully questioning it later, you can find out all the local scandal.

Having enjoyed this book, you may like to read one of the following titles which are available by mail-order *post-free*:-

The Ancient Art of Farting by Dr. C.Huff.
Ever since time began, man (not woman) has farted. Does this ability lie behind many of the so far unexplained mysteries of history ? You Bet - because Dr. C.Huff's research shows conclusively there's something rotten about history taught in schools. If you do most of your reading on the throne, then this book is your ideal companion. Sit back and fart yourself silly as you split your sides laughing!

The Hangover Handbook and Boozer's Bible (in the shape of a beercan).
Ever groaned, burped and cursed the morning after, as Vesuvius erupted in your stomach, a bass drummer thumped on your brain and a canary fouled its nest in your throat? Then you need these 100+ hangover remedies. There's an exclusive Hangover Ratings Chart, a Boozer's Calendar, a Hangover Clinic, and you can meet the Great Drunks of History, try the Boozer's Reading Chart, etc., etc.

The Secret Lives of Teddy Bears (with a FREE jointed Teddy Bear*).
An explanation as to how those annoying little things in life really happen - who hides your keys, who alters your alarm clock and who causes taps to drip. There's also a Teddy Quiz... Bears on Film and Vinyl... Real Life Teddy Bear Facts... Teddy's Timetable... Teddies through History...and a lot more.

How to Get Rid of Your Boss
No matter how much you love your work, there is always one person who makes your professional life a misery - your boss. But all that can change. Find out, with the use of helpful diagrams and cartoons, how to get rid of this person that you despise. It's your chance to get your own back and break free !

The Elvis Spotter's Guide
Strange inconsistencies behind The King's 'death' have lead many fans to believe he is still alive. Now you can track him down with the help of a Priscilla Mask, an instant Elvis Ready Reckoner, 300 amazing Elvis Facts, a 'scoop' of pictures of The King taken since his 'death', cartoons of Elvis in his preferred professions, lists of his favourite meals, cars, girls, etc. And there is a reward of £2 million for the capture of The King. IN COLOUR.

Please return with cheque payment to R&B Publishing, P.O.Box 200, Harrogate, HG29RB
POSTAGE IS FREE within the U.K. Please add £1 per title in other EEC countries and £3 per title elsewhere.
Please send me _____ copies of The Ancient Art of Farting at £3.99 *($A9.95)* each
_____ copies of The Hangover Handbook at £3.99 *($A9.95)* each
_____ copies of The Secret Lives of Teddy Bears at £4.50 *($A9.95)*
_____ copies of How to Get Rid of Your Boss at £3.99 *($A9.95)*each
_____ copies of The Elvis Spotters Guide at £6.99 *($A14.95)* each

Name:_____ Address: _____

_____

_____ Postcode _____

In Australia, please send payment in $A above (which includes postage) to:
MaxiBooks, P.O.Box 268, Springwood, NSW 2777.

*in UK only.